AF358468

THE ULTIMATE
Earthquake
BOOK

BELLANOVA

MELBOURNE · SOFIA · BERLIN

Copyright © 2023 by Jenny Kellett

Earthquakes: The Ultimate Earthquake Book

Visit us at www.bellanovabooks.com

Imprint: Bellanova Books
ISBN: 978-619-264-184-9

CONTENTS

WELCOME TO THE WORLD OF EARTHQUAKES

Welcome, brave explorer, to "The Ultimate Earthquake Book!" You are about to embark on a ground-shaking journey into one of nature's most powerful and fascinating phenomena - earthquakes.

Right now, you might be wondering, what causes the ground beneath our feet to shake? How can we measure the strength of an earthquake? Is there a way to predict when the next big quake will hit? And how have these mighty forces shaped our world, our societies, and even our everyday lives? Don't worry, by the time you turn the last page of this book, you'll have the answers to these questions and so much more!

As you dive into the pages, you'll uncover intriguing stories of how earthquakes have shaped human history, cultures, and our very landscapes. Discover how engineers use innovative designs to combat these powerful natural forces, and explore the intricate links between earthquakes and the environment.

And what's a good adventure without a fun challenge at the end? As you journey through each chapter, keep an eye out for interesting facts, stories, and insights because we've got a challenging quiz waiting for you at the end of the book. It's your chance to show off how much you've learned and become a certified Earthquake Expert!

Ready to embark on this earth-shaking adventure? Strap in, because it's time to feel the rumble and discover the exciting world of earthquakes!

According to the United States Geological Survey (USGS), the Earth has hundreds of thousands of earthquakes annually, but only about 100,000 can be felt, and 100-150 are strong enough to cause damage.

This crack on the Earth's surface was caused by an earthquake.

WHAT IS AN
EARTHQUAKE?

At the most basic level, an earthquake is a natural phenomenon that occurs when stress within the Earth's crust creates seismic waves that reverberate across the planet. Sounds like a bit of a mouthful, doesn't it?

Let's simplify it — imagine you're at a concert, and the crowd is pulsing with energy. Suddenly, the band strikes the first chord, and the crowd goes wild. That's similar to what happens during an earthquake, except the 'crowd' is the Earth's crust, and the 'band' is the built-up stress being released.

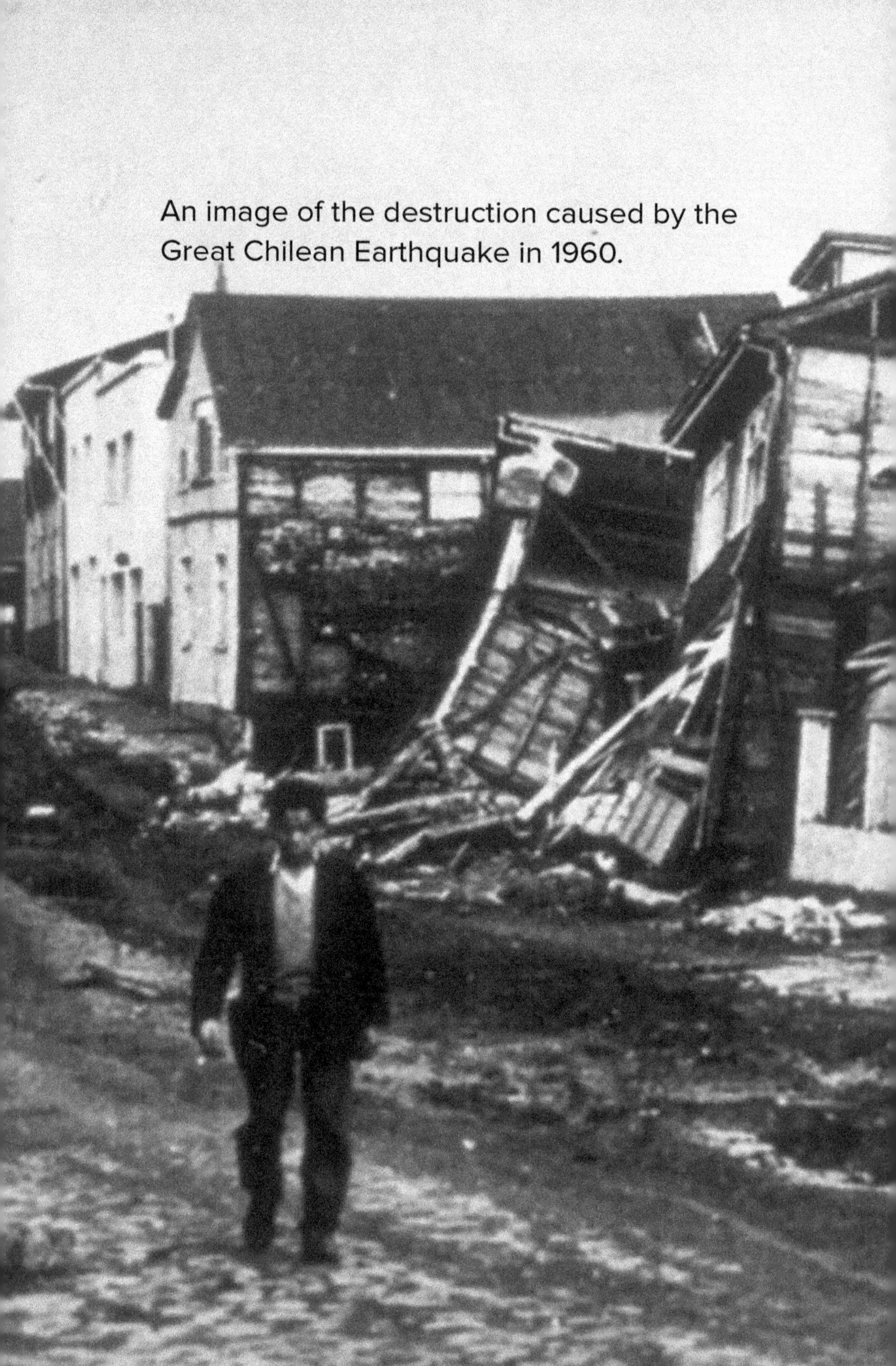

An image of the destruction caused by the Great Chilean Earthquake in 1960.

Not all earthquakes are the same. There are three main types, which are usually categorized by their causes. Let's take a look.

Tectonic Earthquakes

Imagine Earth's crust - the solid outer layer we live on - as a jigsaw puzzle, but with giant pieces called tectonic plates. These plates aren't still; they're always moving, albeit very slowly (about as fast as your fingernails grow!). Sometimes, these plates get stuck at their edges due to friction, but the rest of the plate keeps moving. This builds up a lot of stress, and when the force becomes too much, the rock breaks or slips at the fault line (the cracks where the plates meet), causing an earthquake. These are the most common types of earthquakes we experience.

The world's most powerful recorded earthquake, the Great Chilean Earthquake (Valvidian Earthquake) in 1960, was a tectonic earthquake. It had a magnitude of 9.5, which is about as much energy as 178,000 atomic bombs like the one dropped on Hiroshima!

Volcanic Earthquakes

Now, what if there's a volcano? Underneath a volcano, there's a reservoir of molten rock called **magma**.

When this magma pushes its way to the surface to cause an eruption, it can crack and shake the rocks around it, creating an earthquake. These earthquakes usually occur around areas of volcanic activity and are therefore called volcanic earthquakes.

The island country of Iceland experiences thousands of earthquakes each year because it's right on top of two tectonic plates and has a lot of volcanic activity. In fact, in 2020, a volcano named Fagradalsfjall erupted after thousands of small earthquakes!

Fagradalsfjall volcano erupting in Iceland.

Hoover Dam, Nevada,
USA.

Human-induced Earthquakes

Humans can actually cause earthquakes too, believe it or not! These are often called **induced seismicity**.

When we carry out large-scale activities like filling up huge water reservoirs, extracting oil and gas from underground, or forcing fluids into the ground to break apart rocks for extracting natural gas (a process known as hydraulic fracturing or "fracking"), we can alter the natural stress balance inside Earth's crust. This change in balance can sometimes cause the ground to shake, resulting in an earthquake.

The creation of the Hoover Dam in the United States induced a series of earthquakes in the area during the 1930s. This happened because the massive weight of the water in the new Lake Mead reservoir put pressure on the ground, causing it to adjust and leading to shaking!

INSIDE PLANET EARTH

THE EARTH'S LAYERS: SETTING THE STAGE

To understand how earthquakes happen, we first need to understand what lies beneath the surface of our planet. Our Earth is much more than the surface we see. It's a series of layers, each with unique properties and functions.

The Earth is made up of four layers: the **crust** (the part we live on), the **mantle** below it, and the **inner and outer cores** at the very center.

The crust and the upper part of the mantle form what's known as the **lithosphere**. This isn't one big piece, though—it's broken up into massive slabs called **tectonic plates**. These plates are constantly moving, albeit very slowly, due to the heat from the core and the lower part of the mantle.

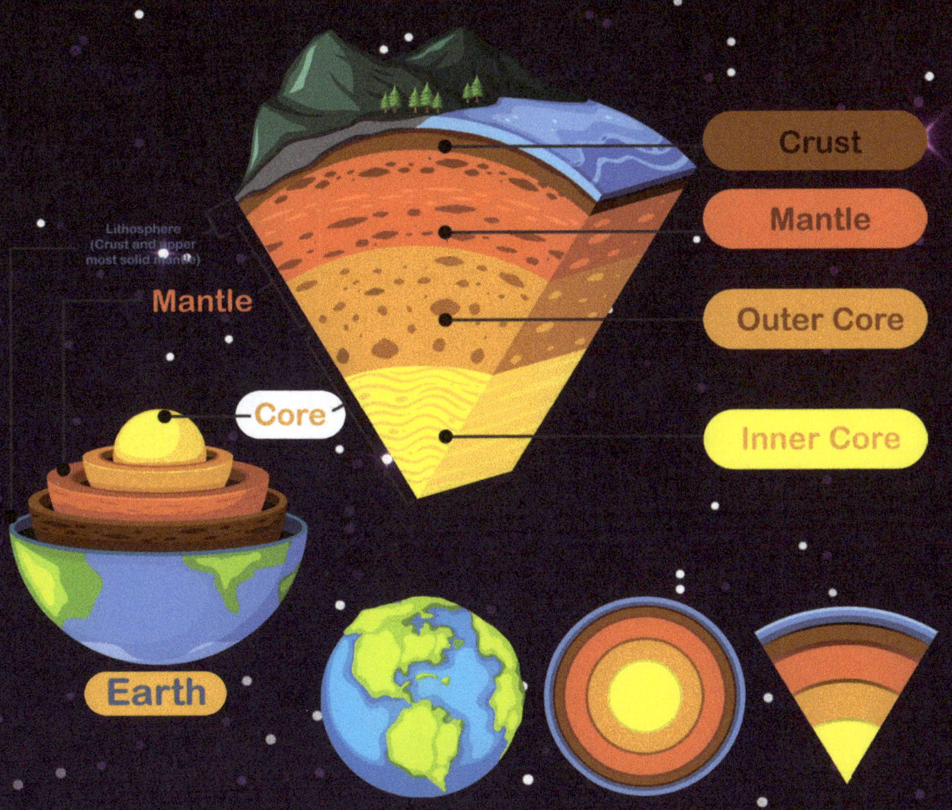

EARTH'S LAYERS

THE ROLE OF TECTONIC PLATES

The birth of an earthquake is deeply connected to the movement of tectonic plates. There are three main types of plate boundaries, each causing different types of earthquakes.

CONVERGENT BOUNDARIES

Where two plates come together, one often gets forced under the other in a process called **subduction**. The subduction process is particularly noteworthy because it's often associated with powerful and destructive earthquakes. In fact, the most powerful earthquakes on Earth, like the Great Chilean Earthquake in 1960, occur in these zones.

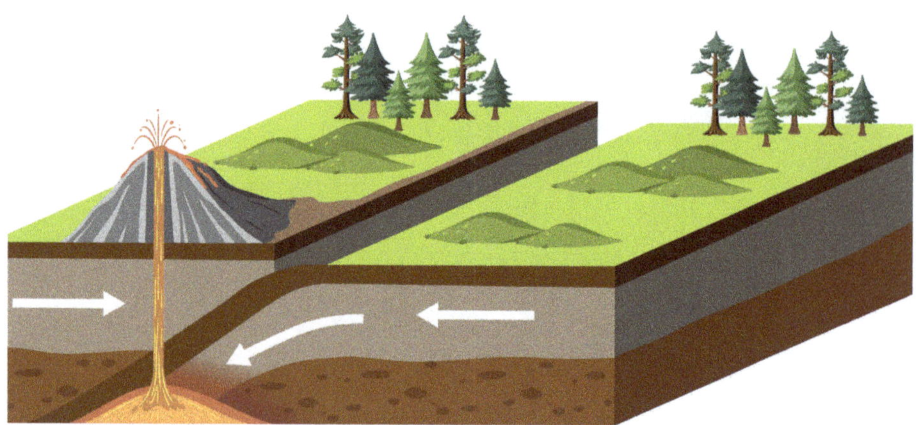

DIVERGENT BOUNDARIES

Where two plates move apart, magma rises to form new crust. While this process is usually less violent than the others, it can still cause earthquakes. The Mid-Atlantic Ridge is a great example, where hundreds of small earthquakes occur every year.

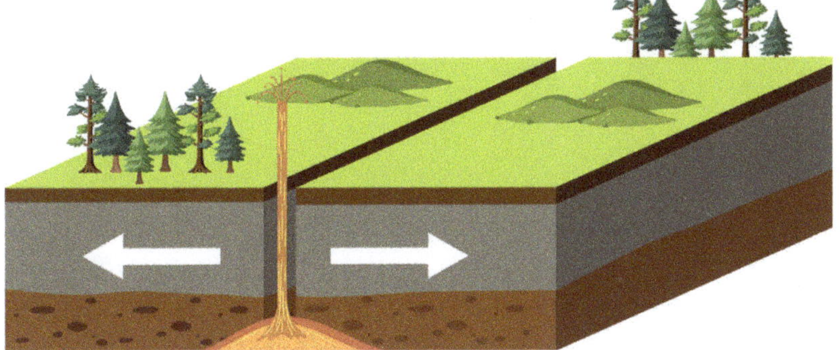

TRANSFORM BOUNDARIES

These are where two plates slide past each other, like cars moving in opposite directions on a highway. They don't diverge or converge, but the sliding isn't smooth due to friction. This causes stress to build up, and when it finally releases, an earthquake occurs. The most famous example is the San Andreas Fault in California.

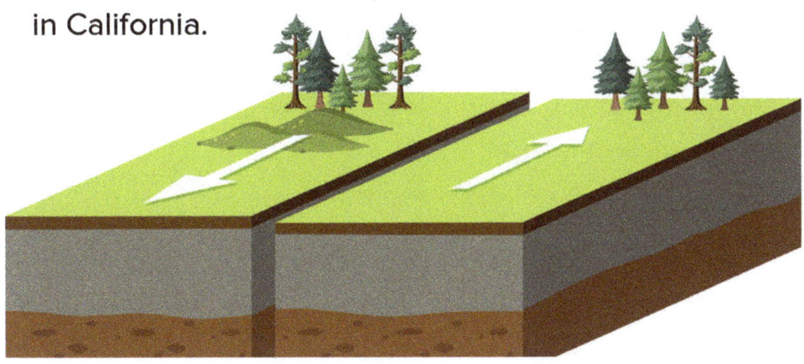

WHY DO EARTHQUAKES HAPPEN?

Now that we've journeyed inside our Earth, it's time to shake things up a bit and understand why earthquakes happen. You see, our Earth isn't as calm and quiet as it appears. It's constantly changing, moving, and reshaping itself. Let's find out how.

SHAKING THINGS UP: THE SCIENCE BEHIND EARTHQUAKES

Earthquakes are the Earth's natural means of releasing stress. When the Earth's plates move against each other, stress builds up at the points where the plates touch (the faults). Over time, this stress can cause the rocks at the fault to deform and eventually, break or slip, releasing energy in the form of **seismic waves**, which we feel as an earthquake.

Think of it as snapping a stick - you bend it (this is the stress) until it breaks (the earthquake) and the energy of the snap sends vibrations (seismic waves) through the stick.

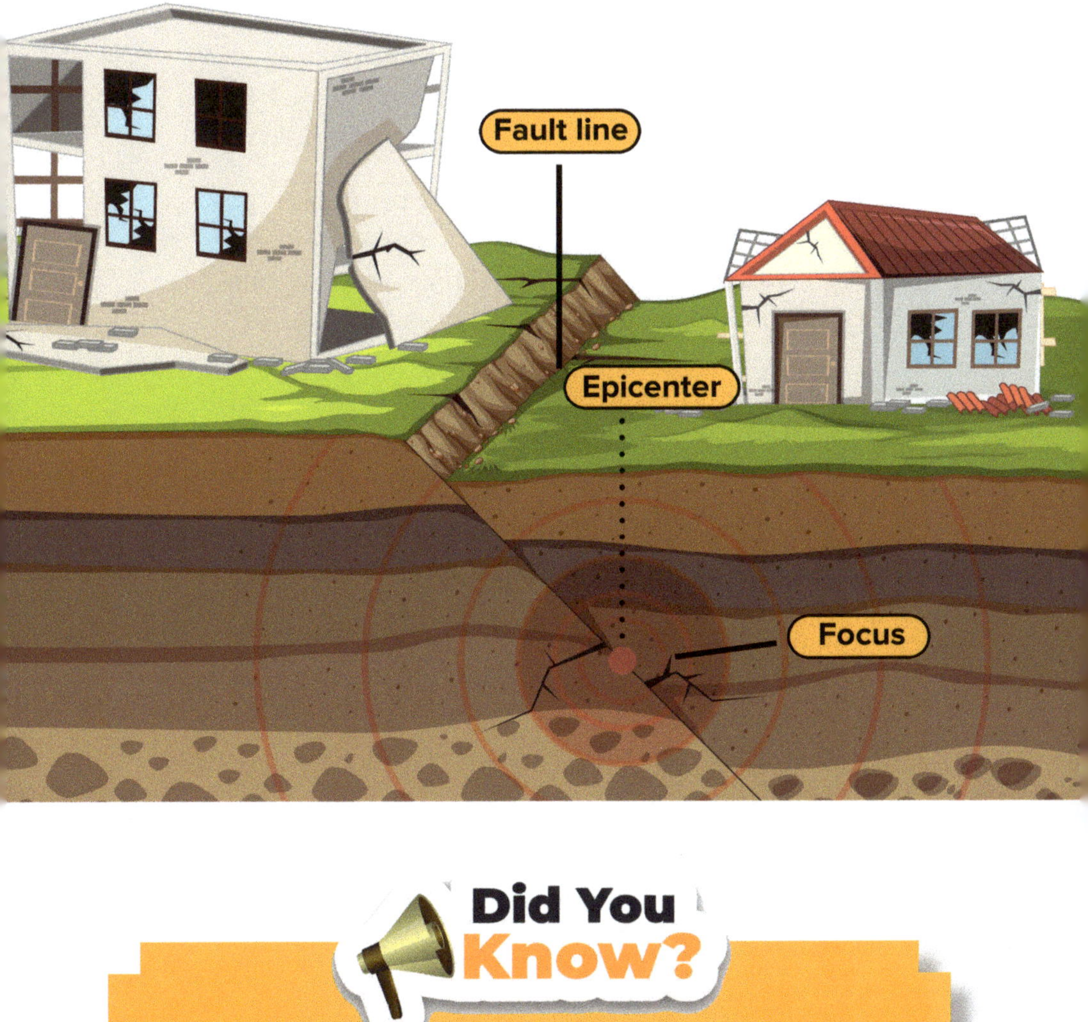

Did You Know?

The point underground where the rocks first break or slip is called the focus or hypocenter of an earthquake. The point directly above it on the Earth's surface is the epicenter.

FAULTS AND SEISMIC WAVES: EARTHQUAKES' DYNAMIC DUO

The Earth's crust is crisscrossed by **faults**, places where blocks of the crust are moving away from each other, towards each other, or sliding past one another. Most earthquakes occur along these fault lines.

When an earthquake happens, it releases energy that travels through the Earth in waves. There are several types of waves, so let's take a closer look.

P-waves (Primary waves)

These are the fastest seismic waves and the first to be detected by seismographs. They move in a push-pull, or compressional, motion — similar to the way sound travels through air. They can travel through solid rock, liquids, and gases.

Animals can often feel the P-waves of an earthquake - which humans can't detect - before the S-waves and surface waves hit. This might be why some animals seem to know an earthquake is coming before humans do.

S-waves (Secondary waves)

These are slower than P-waves and are the second to be recorded by seismographs. They move in a side-to-side or up-and-down, shearing motion, and can only travel through solid material, not through any liquid. This is why S-waves don't reach the parts of the Earth where there's liquid, like the outer core.

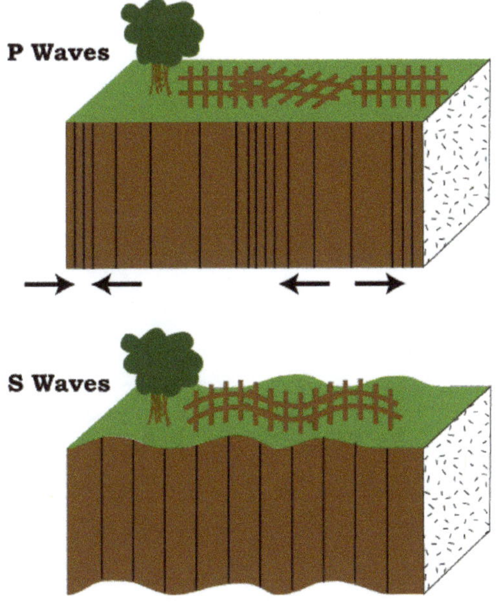

Image: USGS

Surface waves

These waves travel along the Earth's surface and, while they are slower than P-waves and S-waves, they can be far more destructive. Surface waves are responsible for the strong shaking and damage associated with earthquakes. There are two types of surface waves:

- **Love waves** (which move in a horizontal, side-to-side motion); and
- **Rayleigh waves** (which cause both vertical and horizontal ground motion, and are often responsible for the rolling motion felt during an earthquake).

A geophysicist digs a hole for a seismometer at a measuring station on Mount Hood in Oregon, USA. The seismometer, which detects earthquakes, is buried at a depth of at least 1 meter (3 feet).

MEASURING EARTHQUAKES

By now, we know what earthquakes are and why they happen. But how do we measure them? How do we determine whether an earthquake is a light tremble or a major shake-up? Just like we use rulers to measure lengths and thermometers to measure temperature, we have tools to measure earthquakes too.

THE SEISMOGRAPH

Our first step in measuring earthquakes is to detect and record them, and for that, we use an instrument called a **seismograph**. A seismograph records the seismic waves produced by earthquakes, creating an image known as a seismogram.

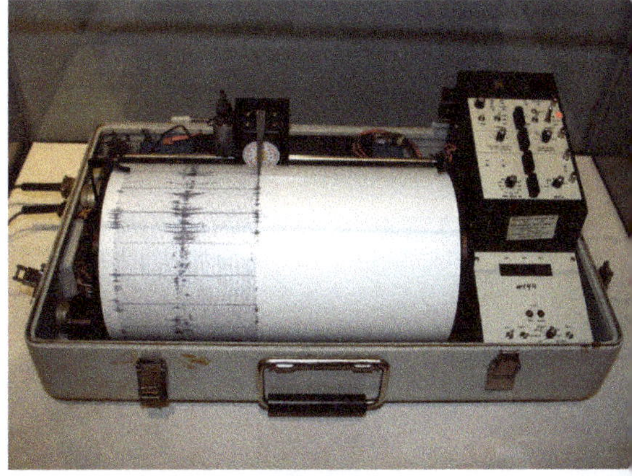

The modern seismograph, however, is much more accurate and complex than the one in the picture. It consists of a large mass, often a weight or a magnet, suspended from a frame. When an earthquake occurs, the frame moves with the shaking Earth and records the movements on a computer.

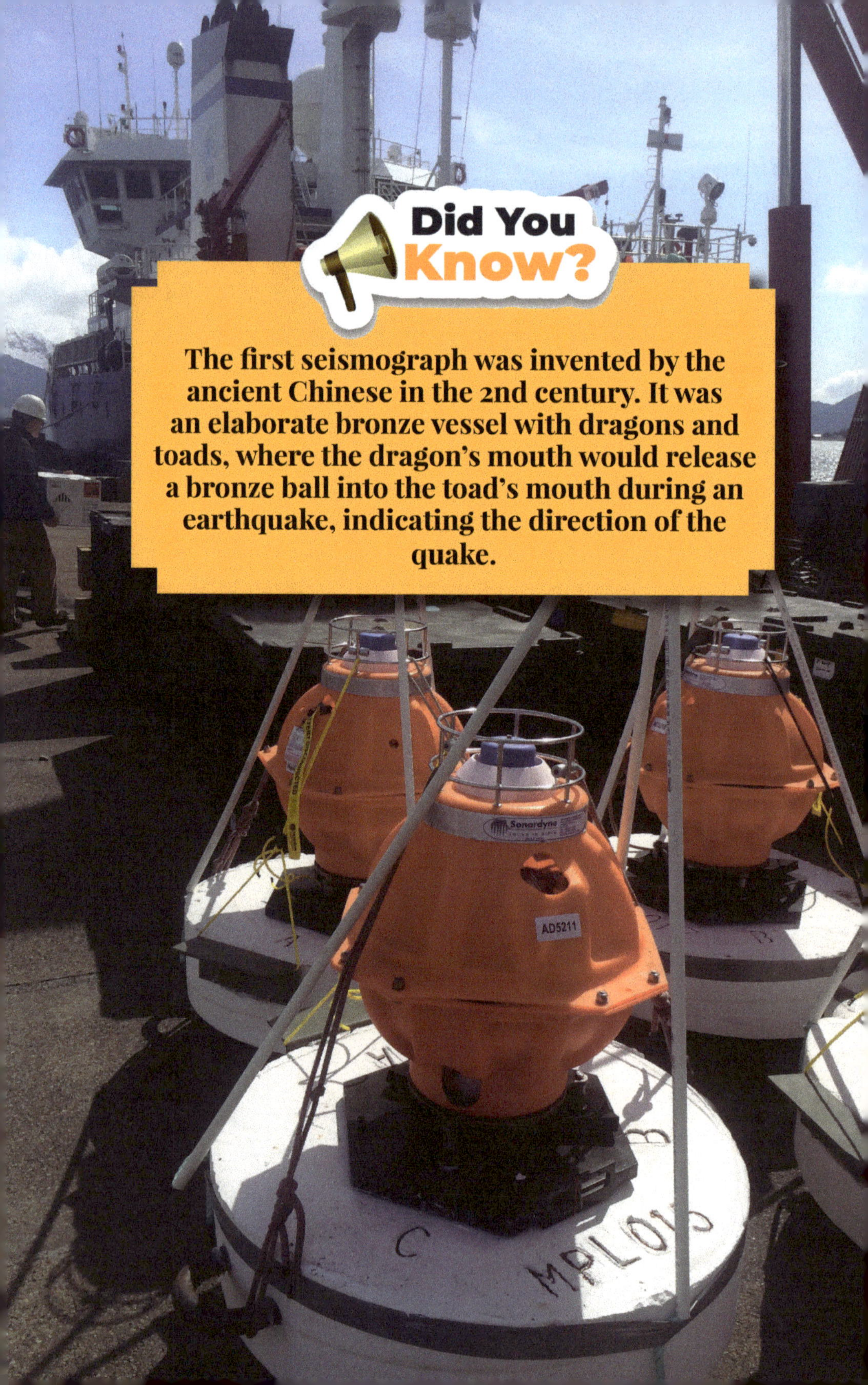

Did You Know?

The first seismograph was invented by the ancient Chinese in the 2nd century. It was an elaborate bronze vessel with dragons and toads, where the dragon's mouth would release a bronze ball into the toad's mouth during an earthquake, indicating the direction of the quake.

THE RICHTER SCALE: NOT JUST A NUMBER

You know how we measure how tall you are, or how much a bag of apples weighs? Well, scientists have ways to measure how strong an earthquake is too. One of the ways they do this was with something called the **Richter scale**, created by Charles F. Richter (pictured) in the 1930s.

The Richter scale uses numbers to show how strong an earthquake is. So, an earthquake might be a 3.0 or a 5.0 on the Richter scale. The bigger the number, the stronger the earthquake. The scale goes up by tens, so a 5.0 earthquake is 10 times stronger in its shaking than a 4.0!

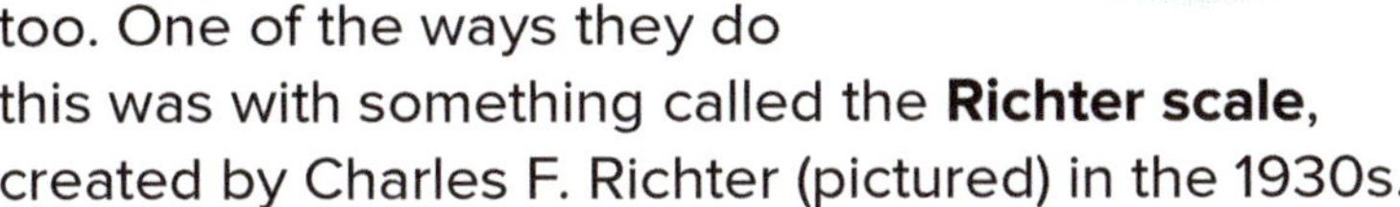

<   These seismometers are heading to the ocean floor to measure earthquake activity in the Gulf of Alaska. Image: USGS

THE MOMENT MAGNITUDE SCALE: A MODERN MEASURE

While the Richter scale is still often used, most scientists now use the **moment magnitude scale (Mw)** for more accurate measurements of large, distant, or deep earthquakes. It does an even better job at telling us how strong an earthquake is.

Just like the Richter scale, the moment magnitude scale also uses numbers to show how strong an earthquake is.

With a grasp of how earthquakes are detected and measured, you've added another powerful tool to your earthquake understanding toolkit. As we move forward, we'll learn about the effects of these quakes and how we can stay safe when they occur. So, hold on tight; the journey continues!

The smallest earthquakes, those below 3.0 on the moment magnitude scale, are called microearthquakes. They occur globally every day and are not usually felt by humans.

The Magnitude of an Earthquake

EARTHQUAKES
IN HISTORY

Throughout history, earthquakes have shaped our world, both literally and metaphorically. They've carved our landscapes, spurred scientific advances, and influenced how societies prepare for natural disasters. Let's travel back in time and revisit some of the most significant earthquakes in history.

THE SAN FRANCISCO EARTHQUAKE, 1906

The morning of April 18, 1906, was not like any other for the residents of San Francisco. The San Andreas Fault slipped along a segment about 290 miles long, unleashing an earthquake estimated at a magnitude of 7.9.

The impact was catastrophic - fires raged across the city for days, leading to the destruction of over 80% of San Francisco. But out of this tragedy came one of the most important investigations in the history of seismology, the Lawson Report. This study advanced our understanding of earthquakes and was crucial in the development of the theory of plate tectonics.

THE GREAT CHILEAN EARTHQUAKE, 1960

No discussion of earthquakes can exclude the Great Chilean Earthquake of May 22, 1960. Clocking in at an astonishing magnitude of 9.5, it remains the most powerful earthquake ever recorded. The earthquake, along with the resulting tsunamis and landslides, caused extensive damage and loss of life.

This event brought worldwide attention to the seismic hazard posed by subduction zones (where one tectonic plate is forced under another), leading to increased global efforts in earthquake preparedness and tsunami warning systems.

The effects of the earthquake were felt as far away as Hawaii and Japan, where the earthquake caused huge tsunamis, as can be seen in this photo from Hilo, Hawaii.

THE HAITI EARTHQUAKE, 2010

A catastrophic magnitude 7.0 earthquake struck Haiti on January 12, 2010, devastating the capital, Port-au-Prince. With weak infrastructure and a lack of local resources, the country struggled with the aftermath of the quake.

Haiti's earthquake reminded the world of the severe impacts earthquakes can have on society, especially in countries lacking sufficient preparation and resources. This earthquake triggered an international discussion on improving global assistance strategies for natural disasters, particularly in developing countries.

RSALOĞLU
BALKON
BALKON
MUT

TURKEY-SYRIA EARTHQUAKE, 2023

On 26 January, 2023, a 7.8 magnitude earthquake hit southern and central Turkey and northern and western Syria, where the Arabian and Anatolian tectonic plates meet. Around 14 million people were affected by the earthquake, with about 1.5 million left homeless.

Nearly 60,000 people lost their lives in the earthquake, which was one of the largest ever to hit the region. Volunteers from all around the world went to Turkey and Syria to help search for survivors and care for the injured and homeless.

In the three months following the earthquake, there were over 30,000 aftershocks.

THE IMPACT OF
EARTHQUAKES

In our journey to understand earthquakes, we've delved into why they happen, how we measure them, and significant quakes from the past. Now, let's explore what happens when the shaking stops - the immediate and long-term effects of earthquakes, the geological landforms they create, and the secondary hazards they can trigger.

When an earthquake strikes, its immediate effects can be both terrifying and devastating. The shaking ground can cause buildings and other structures to collapse, roads and bridges to buckle, and utilities such as electricity, gas, and water services to be disrupted. These immediate impacts can cause injuries and loss of life, and pose significant challenges for emergency services.

During the 1985 Mexico City earthquake (pictured), some buildings collapsed while others nearby remained standing. This was due to a phenomenon known as seismic amplification – some parts of the city were built on old lakebed sediments, which amplified the shaking.

SECONDARY HAZARDS: EARTHQUAKES' DANGEROUS DOMINO EFFECTS

The shaking doesn't have to stop for the danger to continue. Earthquakes often trigger secondary hazards such as landslides, tsunamis, and even fires.

LANDSLIDES: When earthquakes shake loose ground on slopes, they can trigger landslides. These sudden and rapid slides of a mass of rock, earth, or debris down a slope can cause additional destruction in areas already affected by the quake.

TSUNAMIS: Submarine earthquakes, those that occur under the ocean floor, can displace large amounts of water and generate tsunamis. These huge sea waves can travel vast distances, causing destruction far from the earthquake's epicenter.

Aftermath of the 2004 Indian Ocean tsunami, triggered by an earthquake.

A landslide in the USA.

FIRES: Fires after earthquakes can be particularly devastating. Broken gas lines and downed power lines can spark fires, while disrupted water lines can hamper firefighting efforts.

Did You Know?

The 1906 San Francisco earthquake is a classic example of secondary hazards. While the quake caused considerable damage, it was the subsequent city-wide fires, fueled by broken gas lines and unable to be fought due to broken water mains, that caused the most destruction.

The impacts of an earthquake can extend far beyond the event itself. Areas hit by large earthquakes often face long-term effects such as changes to the landscape, economic loss, and societal shifts.

Large earthquakes can cause permanent changes to the Earth's surface, changes in the course of rivers, and even the creation of new landforms like lakes and hills.

The economic impact of a major earthquake can be significant, with costs for rebuilding infrastructure, homes, and businesses, and providing support for displaced people. These impacts can last for many years after the earthquake.

Societal changes are often seen too. Earthquakes can lead to population movements, changes in living conditions, and renewed emphasis on disaster preparedness and building codes.

Earthquakes may only last a few seconds or minutes, but their effects can be felt for years, even generations.

The 1964 Alaska earthquake (pictured) caused parts of the coastline to rise by up to 38 feet, while other areas sunk by several feet. This dramatically altered the landscape and impacted local ecosystems.

As well as the effects on humans living in areas devastated by earthquakes, they also have an important role in shaping our planet.

Mountain Formation

When tectonic plates collide and push against each other (like in a convergent boundary), it can cause the crust to crumple and fold, leading to the formation of mountain ranges. The majestic Himalayas, for instance, were formed from the collision of the Indian and Eurasian Plates.

Fun Fact: *The Himalayas (pictured) continue to grow about 2.4 inches each year due to tectonic forces!*

Rift Valleys and Fissures

When plates move apart (like in a divergent boundary), the land can sink down between them, forming a valley. The Great Rift Valley in Africa is an example of a large rift valley caused by divergent tectonic plates.

Fun Fact: *The Great Rift Valley is over 6,000 kilometers long and spans two continents — Africa and Asia!*

Fault Scarps

Sometimes, an earthquake's shaking causes a sudden shift along a fault, creating a step or small cliff in the landscape known as a fault scarp.

Fun Fact: *The 1959 Hebgen Lake earthquake in Montana caused a massive fault scarp over 20 feet high!*

Earthquake Lakes

Sometimes, landslides triggered by earthquakes can block rivers, forming natural dams. Over time, these blocked rivers can turn into serene, beautiful earthquake lakes.

Fun Fact: China's Tangjiashan Lake was formed by a deadly earthquake in 2008 and has since become a tourist spot.

Remember, the Earth has been changing and evolving for billions of years, and earthquakes are a natural part of that process. They help shape the breathtaking landscapes that make our planet so unique. So, while they can be destructive, earthquakes also contribute to the ever-changing beauty of Mother Earth.

Quake Lake (pictured) is an earthquake lake formed after the deadly 1959 earthquake in Montana, USA. Image: *James St. John*

As well as long-term effects on the shape of our planet, earthquakes can directly impact various ecosystems, making life very difficult for a range of creatures—not just humans.

Landforms

Earthquakes can cause landslides, avalanches (pictured), or even change the course of rivers, affecting the habitats of many plant and animal species.

Aquatic Life

Underwater earthquakes can impact marine ecosystems by causing tsunamis and changes in the seafloor that can disrupt marine habitats.

Animal Behavior

Interestingly, some animals seem to have the ability to sense an impending earthquake, exhibiting unusual behaviors before the shaking begins.

Did You Know?

Before the 2004 Indian Ocean earthquake and tsunami, elephants in Sri Lanka and Thailand were reported to have moved to higher ground before the tsunami hit.

SURVIVING AN EARTHQUAKE

While predicting earthquakes may remain a work in progress, one thing we can do is prepare for them. Being well-prepared can make a significant difference in our ability to survive and recover from these natural disasters. Let's take a look at some handy tips and techniques for ensuring safety before, during, and after an earthquake.

The Great ShakeOut, a global earthquake preparedness event, conducts simultaneous earthquake drills worldwide to encourage everyone to practice how to be safe during earthquakes.

Getting ready before an earthquake strikes is crucial to minimize damage and ensure your safety and that of your loved ones.

Secure Your Home

Anchor heavy furniture, secure appliances, and hang heavy items like mirrors and paintings away from beds, couches, and anywhere people sit or sleep.

Emergency Kit

Prepare an emergency kit with essential items such as water, non-perishable food, a first-aid kit, a flashlight, a portable radio, extra batteries, and important documents.

Create a Plan

Develop a family emergency plan. This should include a safe place to meet after the quake and a person to contact outside of your area who can relay messages.

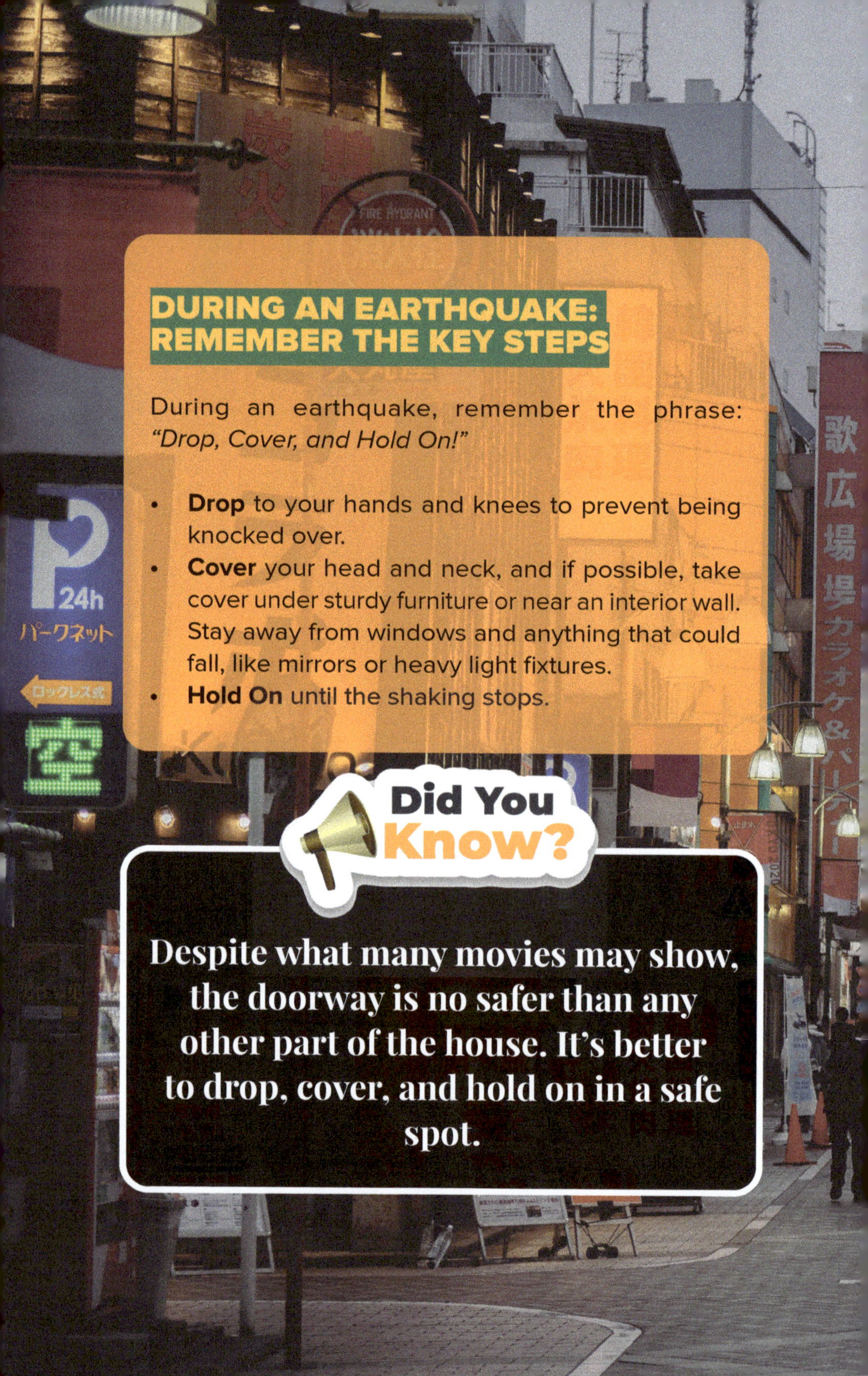

DURING AN EARTHQUAKE: REMEMBER THE KEY STEPS

During an earthquake, remember the phrase: *"Drop, Cover, and Hold On!"*

- **Drop** to your hands and knees to prevent being knocked over.
- **Cover** your head and neck, and if possible, take cover under sturdy furniture or near an interior wall. Stay away from windows and anything that could fall, like mirrors or heavy light fixtures.
- **Hold On** until the shaking stops.

Did You Know?

Despite what many movies may show, the doorway is no safer than any other part of the house. It's better to drop, cover, and hold on in a safe spot.

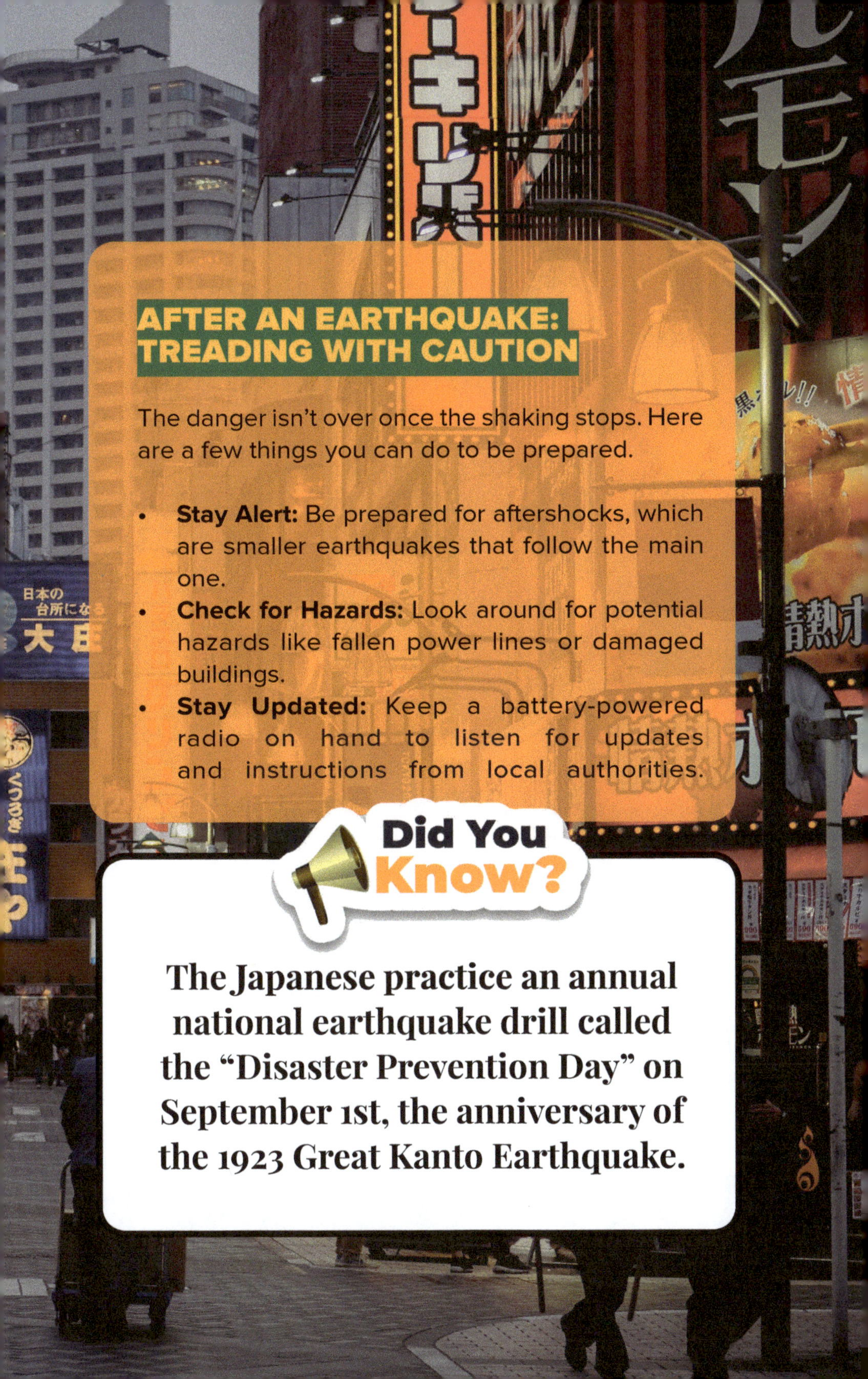

AFTER AN EARTHQUAKE: TREADING WITH CAUTION

The danger isn't over once the shaking stops. Here are a few things you can do to be prepared.

- **Stay Alert:** Be prepared for aftershocks, which are smaller earthquakes that follow the main one.
- **Check for Hazards:** Look around for potential hazards like fallen power lines or damaged buildings.
- **Stay Updated:** Keep a battery-powered radio on hand to listen for updates and instructions from local authorities.

Did You Know?

The Japanese practice an annual national earthquake drill called the "Disaster Prevention Day" on September 1st, the anniversary of the 1923 Great Kanto Earthquake.

Did You Know?
The Transamerica Pyramid in San Francisco (pictured) uses a form of base isolation. Its wide base tapers into a narrow top, which helps it sway safely during earthquakes.

BUILDING FOR EARTHQUAKES

While earthquakes are indeed powerful forces of nature, did you know we can actually design our buildings and infrastructure to withstand their mighty shakes? Let's journey into the world of engineering and discover how we can build to beat earthquakes.

THE SCIENCE BEHIND THE SHAKES: EARTHQUAKE-RESISTANT DESIGN

When engineers design buildings and other structures to resist earthquakes, they need to understand the way buildings react to ground shaking. They consider factors like building material, height, shape, and the soil beneath.

Building Techniques

BASE ISOLATION

This technique involves separating the building from the ground using flexible bearings or pads (pictured right), known as base isolators. During an earthquake, the isolators absorb much of the shock, allowing the building to remain stable.

DAMPING

Dampers are devices (left) that absorb energy, reducing the amount of energy transferred to the building during an earthquake and thus, the shaking the building experiences. Think of it like shock absorbers in a car, absorbing the bumps on the road.

SHAPE AND MATERIAL CHOICES

The shape of a building and the materials used can greatly influence how it responds to an earthquake. Buildings made of flexible materials like wood and steel or shaped in regular, symmetrical forms are more likely to withstand an earthquake's forces.

STRENGTHENING OUR STRUCTURES

As our understanding of earthquakes evolves, so too does our approach to designing and building structures that can withstand them. Engineers and scientists continually work together, employing advanced computer simulations, wind tunnel testing, and **shake table** (a device used by engineers and scientists to simulate the shaking and rattling of earthquakes in a controlled laboratory) experiments to develop and refine earthquake-resistant design techniques.

Did You Know?

Japan's E-Defense, the world's largest shake table, can simulate the motions of the most devastating earthquakes. It allows engineers to test full-sized buildings under earthquake-like conditions.

THE FUTURE OF EARTHQUAKES

As we close this earth-shaking adventure, let's look towards the future. What does it hold for the science of earthquakes? With cutting-edge technology, novel research developments, and even a potential link to climate change, the future of earthquake science is as dynamic as the quakes themselves.

NEXT-GENERATION DETECTION: TECHNOLOGICAL ADVANCES

Modern technology is giving us new and exciting ways to detect and study earthquakes. Here's a peek into a few exciting developments:

EARTHQUAKE EARLY WARNING SYSTEMS (EEWS): These systems use the first waves (P-waves) from an earthquake, which travel faster than the damaging waves, to provide a warning before the shaking starts. While it may only provide seconds to minutes of warning, this can be crucial for taking protective actions.

ARTIFICIAL INTELLIGENCE (AI) IN EARTHQUAKE DETECTION

AI technologies are being utilized to quickly analyze seismic data, helping to more accurately locate earthquakes and assess their magnitude.

SATELLITE TECHNOLOGY

Satellites are being used to monitor tectonic movements from space, providing valuable data on seismic activity.

The ShakeAlert system in the United States uses ground motion sensors to detect earthquakes and send alerts to people's phones before the shaking reaches them.

CLIMATE CHANGE AND EARTHQUAKES: AN EMERGING CONNECTION?

As we come to terms with the realities of a changing climate, scientists are exploring possible links between climate change and earthquakes. The idea is still under investigation, but here's the current thinking:

MELTING GLACIERS AND RISING SEAS

The melting of ice sheets and glaciers, as well as rising sea levels due to climate change, can alter the pressure on the Earth's crust, potentially triggering seismic activity.

HUMAN ACTIVITIES

Activities like hydraulic fracturing (fracking) and reservoir-induced seismicity (earthquakes triggered by the filling of large reservoirs behind dams) can trigger seismic activity.

While the connection is not fully understood, this is an active area of research, highlighting how interconnected our Earth systems are.

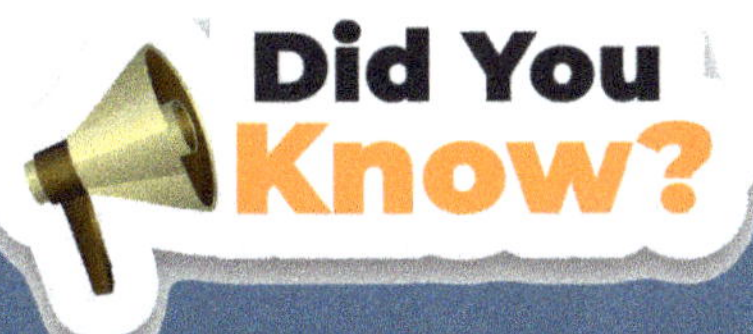

The phenomenon of human-induced earthquakes is sometimes referred to as "anthroposeismic" activity, from 'anthropo-' for 'human' and '-seismic' for 'earthquake'.

As we continue to improve our understanding of earthquakes, we stand better prepared to handle their impacts and safeguard our societies. The more we learn, the more equipped we become to live in harmony with these powerful natural events. From the depths of the Earth's core to the cutting edge of technology, the journey through the world of earthquakes is truly a thrilling ride.

EARTHQUAKE
FACTS

Just when you thought you knew all there is to know about earthquakes, there's more! Afterwards, test yourself in our earthquake quiz.

The Earth experiences an earthquake roughly every 15 minutes, but most are too small to feel.

● ● ●

Earthquakes can occur anywhere, but they are most likely to strike along tectonic plate boundaries.

● ● ●

Large earthquakes can cause the Earth to vibrate, similar to the ringing of a bell, for days.

● ● ●

The smallest earthquake ever recorded was -3 on the Richter scale, which is extremely minor.

The energy of earthquakes is estimated using a unit called a "joule". The 2011 Japan earthquake is estimated to have released 3.9 x 10^22 joules of energy!

•••

The moon also experiences quakes, referred to as "moonquakes." They are believed to occur due to the gravitational interaction with Earth, and astronauts are trained to deal with them.

•••

The first "pendulum seismoscope" to measure the shaking during an earthquake was developed in 1751, and it wasn't until 1855 that faults were recognized as the source of earthquakes.

•••

Alaska is the most earthquake-prone state in the U.S. and one of the most seismically active regions globally.

The Himalayan mountain range, including Mount Everest, was formed due to tectonic activity that still causes many of the earthquakes in India today.

•••

The deadliest earthquake in recorded history occurred in central China in 1556. The majority of people in the area lived in caves carved from soft rock, leading to a catastrophic collapse during the quake.

•••

Most earthquakes occur within 50 miles of the Earth's surface. That's relatively close considering Earth's radius is about 4,000 miles!

•••

The San Andreas Fault in California is constantly moving at a rate of about 2 inches per year, approximately the same speed as our fingernail grows. This means that Los Angeles and San Francisco will be next-door neighbors in about 15 million years!

•••

Earthquakes under the ocean can trigger tsunamis by causing landslides on the ocean floor.

The United States Geological Survey (USGS) runs the "Did You Feel It?" program. It's a citizen science project that allows people to report their experiences of an earthquake through an online form, helping scientists gather data on earthquakes in the U.S.

• • •

Significant earthquakes can alter the Earth's axis. The 2011 earthquake in Japan, which caused a devastating tsunami, shifted Earth's axis by as much as 10 inches, and changed the speed of the planet's rotation.

• • •

The Great Alaskan Earthquake of 1964 (pictured) lasted for about 4 minutes - an incredibly long duration for an earthquake.

The 1906 San Francisco Earthquake was the deadliest in U.S. history, mainly due to fires that raged on for several days.

• • •

The energy release from a major earthquake can exceed that of the first atomic bomb.

• • •

Before seismographs, the Italians used bells to detect earthquakes, similar to the ancient Chinese. They also used 'earthquake architecture' to protect their buildings during earthquakes.

• • •

"Quake lakes" are lakes created by landslides or debris flow caused by an earthquake. These can be temporary or permanent.

• • •

Earthquakes can sometimes turn water-saturated sand and silt into a liquid in a process known as liquefaction, causing buildings and other structures to sink.

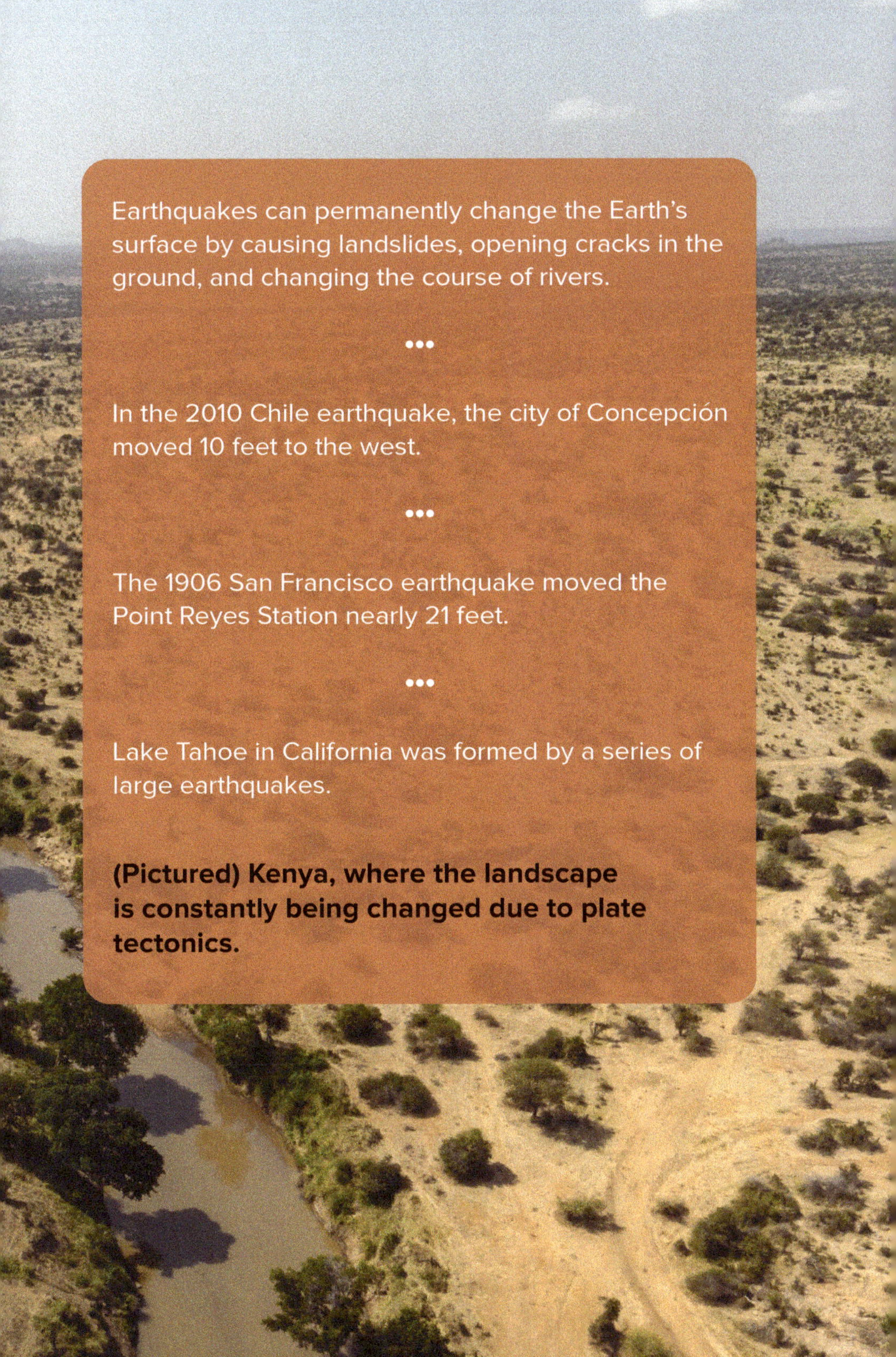

Earthquakes can permanently change the Earth's surface by causing landslides, opening cracks in the ground, and changing the course of rivers.

•••

In the 2010 Chile earthquake, the city of Concepción moved 10 feet to the west.

•••

The 1906 San Francisco earthquake moved the Point Reyes Station nearly 21 feet.

•••

Lake Tahoe in California was formed by a series of large earthquakes.

(Pictured) Kenya, where the landscape is constantly being changed due to plate tectonics.

An earthquake in the Indian Ocean in 2004 triggered tsunamis that killed around 230,000 people in 14 countries. The 2004 Indian Ocean earthquake was so powerful it even caused the Earth to vibrate as much as 0.39 in (1 cm).

•••

In 1811 and 1812, the town of New Madrid in Missouri experienced a series of intense earthquakes that were felt as far away as Boston and Denver.

•••

An earthquake's effects can be felt far beyond the epicenter. For example, the 1906 earthquake in Valparaíso, Chile, caused a tsunami that reached Hawaii, Japan, and the Philippines.

•••

In the 1976 Tangshan earthquake in China, an estimated 242,000 to 655,000 people were killed, making it one of the deadliest in history.

•••

Japan is one of the world's most earthquake-prone countries due to its location in the Ring of Fire, an area with a high number of earthquakes and volcanic eruptions. The Ring of Fire is associated with a direct line of subduction zones, and about 81% of the world's largest earthquakes occur along it.

•••

Sometimes small earthquakes, known as foreshocks, can occur before a large earthquake.

•••

The depth of an earthquake can greatly influence the damage it causes on the surface. Shallow earthquakes tend to be more damaging than deep ones.

•••

There are regions known as seismic gaps where no significant seismic activity has occurred for a long time. These are often the sites of major earthquakes when they finally happen.

•••

New Zealand (pictured) experiences thousands of earthquakes each year, but only about 200 are felt by people.

Earthquakes can sometimes cause a phenomenon called **earthquake lights**, where the stress of tectonic activity generates electric charges that light up the sky.

•••

The Great Wall of China was built along a seismic fault, and some sections have been damaged by earthquakes over the centuries.

•••

Many seismologists use a globe to demonstrate plate tectonics because the Earth's surface is curved, not flat. This shows how the plates can slide under one another.

•••

When an earthquake happens, the seismic waves it sends out are similar to the ripples in a pond when you throw a rock into it.

•••

The Indian plate is still moving at 2.6 in (67 mm) per year, and over the next 10 million years it will travel about 1,500 kilometers (932 miles) into Asia.

The Great Wall of China.

The April 2015 Nepal earthquake triggered an avalanche on Mount Everest, killing 21 climbers and making it the deadliest day on the mountain.

•••

Humans can cause earthquakes, too. Activities such as damming rivers, mining fossil fuels, and injecting wastewater deep into the ground can induce earthquakes.

•••

More earthquakes occur in the northern hemisphere than the southern hemisphere.

•••

There is a theory called "Earthquake Weather" that originated in ancient Greece, suggesting that earthquakes are more common during hot and calm weather, but studies have found no correlation between weather and earthquakes.

The word "seismograph" comes from two Greek words meaning to shake (seismos) and to write (graphein).

●●●

The deepest earthquake ever recorded was in Bolivia at a depth of 467 miles (750 kilometers) in 1994.

●●●

The longest earthquake rupture ever recorded was the 2004 Sumatra earthquake that lasted between 500 and 600 seconds. It caused one of the deadliest tsunamis in history.

●●●

Many dinosaur fossils are found in Earth's seismic hot spots, leading some scientists to believe that earthquakes may have played a role in their extinction.

The first earthquake for which an accurate epicenter was determined was the 1833 Sumatra earthquake.

•••

Some animals, such as dogs and cats, appear to behave unusually up to a few days before an earthquake occurs.

•••

Geysers and hot springs can be influenced by seismic activity. The famous Old Faithful Geyser (pictured) in Yellowstone National Park varies its eruptions due to earthquakes.

•••

In Ancient times, people believed earthquakes were caused by huge animals, angry gods, or giants shaking the Earth.

•••

In the 4th Century BC, the Greek philosopher Aristotle suggested that earthquakes were caused by winds trapped in subterranean caves.

Old Faithful Geyser in Yellowstone
National Park.

Mount Fuji, Japan.

Earthquake-prone Japan is home to 10% of the world's active volcanoes.

• • •

The first scientifically explained earthquake occurred in Lisbon, Portugal, on November 1, 1755. The Lisbon earthquake led to the modern science of seismology.

• • •

While Hollywood often depicts gaping, bottomless cracks opening in the Earth during earthquakes, this is largely a myth.

• • •

A "slow earthquake" is a type of quake that releases its built-up energy over hours or even days, rather than in a few catastrophic seconds or minutes.

• • •

An earthquake can change the length of a day by milliseconds by shifting the distribution of the Earth's mass.

• • •

Rotorua, New Zealand experiences over 15,000 earthquakes per year, but only about 100-150 are strong enough to be felt.

EARTHQUAKE *Quiz*

So you think you're an earthquake expert now?! Let's find out! Answers are on the following page.

1. What are the three types of earthquakes mentioned in this book?

2. How does the 'Ring of Fire' relate to earthquakes?

3. What is an example of a transform boundary, and how does it relate to earthquakes?

4. Name two different ways that old civilizations used to record or cope with earthquakes.

5. What are the 3 types of seismic waves, and how do they relate to earthquakes?

6 What is the difference between the Richter scale and the Moment Magnitude Scale?

7 Which earthquake was the most powerful ever recorded, and where did it occur?

8 What happened on February 6, 2023, in Turkey and Syria?

9 What is an example of a geological landform that can be created by earthquakes?

10 What's the difference between the three types of tectonic plate boundaries, and how does each relate to earthquakes?

11 What is the process of liquefaction, and when can it occur?

12 What is a tsunami and how can it be caused by an earthquake?

13 Can earthquakes be predicted? Explain your answer.

14 Name three safety tips for surviving an earthquake.

15 How do engineers design buildings to withstand earthquakes?

16 Give an example of how an earthquake has influenced human civilization.

17 What are the immediate and long-term effects of an earthquake on an environment?

18 How might climate change potentially be linked to earthquakes?

Indonesia experiences around
10,000 earthquakes a year.

A thermal spring and geyser in Iceland.

19 Which city experiences over 15,000 earthquakes per year, but only about 100-150 are strong enough to be felt?

20 Name one way that seismic activity can affect geysers and hot springs.

21 What's a "moonquake," and who might need to be prepared for one?

22 How does the process of subduction relate to earthquakes?

23 What is the "Did You Feel It?" program, and who runs it?

24 What is the connection between fracking and earthquakes?

25 Why do so many earthquakes occur in Japan?

ANSWERS

1. Tectonic, volcanic, and human-induced (or induced seismicity).
2. The 'Ring of Fire' is a major area in the basin of the Pacific Ocean where many earthquakes and volcanic eruptions occur due to tectonic plate boundaries.
3. The San Andreas Fault in California is an example of a transform boundary, where two tectonic plates slide past each other, often causing earthquakes.
4. The ancient Chinese used a seismoscope, and the ancient Italians used 'earthquake architecture,' designing buildings that could withstand tremors.
5. P-waves are push-pull waves and are the fastest seismic waves. S-waves shake the ground back and forth. Surface waves cause most of the shaking during an earthquake.
6. The Richter scale measures the amplitude of seismic waves, while the Moment Magnitude Scale measures the total energy released by an earthquake.
7. The most powerful earthquake ever recorded was a 9.5 magnitude quake in Valdivia, Chile in 1960.
8. The February 6, 2023, earthquake in Turkey resulted in significant casualties and damage, including nearly 60,000 deaths.
9. An example of a geological landform created by an earthquake is a fault scarp.
10. Divergent boundaries occur where two plates move apart, convergent boundaries where they come together, and transform boundaries where they slide past each other. All these movements can cause earthquakes.

11. Liquefaction is a process by which water-saturated sediment temporarily loses strength and acts as a fluid, like when you wiggle your toes in the wet sand near the water at the beach. This can occur during the intense shaking of an earthquake.
12. A tsunami is a series of sea waves usually caused by displacement of the ocean floor. Earthquakes are a common cause of this displacement.
13. Currently, we can't predict exactly when and where an earthquake will occur. However, scientists are working on understanding patterns and signs to better anticipate future earthquakes.
14. Safety tips include: Drop, cover, and hold on during the quake; have a preparedness kit; and participate in regular earthquake drills.
15. Engineers use a variety of techniques, including base isolation and energy dissipation devices, to design buildings that can resist the forces generated by earthquakes.
16. The 1755 Lisbon earthquake, for example, significantly influenced European art and philosophy and led to the first attempts at modern seismology.
17. Immediate effects might include landslides and tsunamis, while long-term effects might include changes to the landscape and the local ecosystem.
18. Climate change could potentially affect earthquakes by causing changes in groundwater or permafrost, altering pressures on the Earth's crust, though this is still a topic of research.

19. Rotorua, New Zealand experiences over 15,000 earthquakes per year, but only about 100-150 are strong enough to be felt.

20. Seismic activity can cause changes in the eruption patterns of geysers and the flow of hot springs. For example, the Old Faithful Geyser in Yellowstone National Park varies its eruptions due to earthquakes.

21. A 'moonquake' is an earthquake on the Moon, and astronauts need to be prepared for them in case they occur during lunar missions.

22. Subduction is a geological process that occurs at convergent boundaries where one tectonic plate is forced under another. This movement can cause intense pressure to build up over time. When the stress becomes too great, it's released in the form of an earthquake.

23. The "Did You Feel It?" program is run by the United States Geological Survey (USGS). It's a citizen science project that allows people to report their experiences of an earthquake through an online form, helping scientists gather data on earthquakes in the U.S.

24. Fracking, or hydraulic fracturing, is a process used to extract natural gas and oil from deep rock formations. It involves injecting water, sand, and chemicals into a well under high pressure to fracture the rocks and release the gas or oil. This process can induce seismic activity, creating what are known as induced earthquakes.

25. Japan is located along the "Ring of Fire," an area with many active faults and tectonic plate boundaries. Because of this, the country is highly seismic and experiences frequent earthquakes. Additionally, the subduction of the Pacific Plate beneath the Eurasian Plate results in significant tectonic activity.

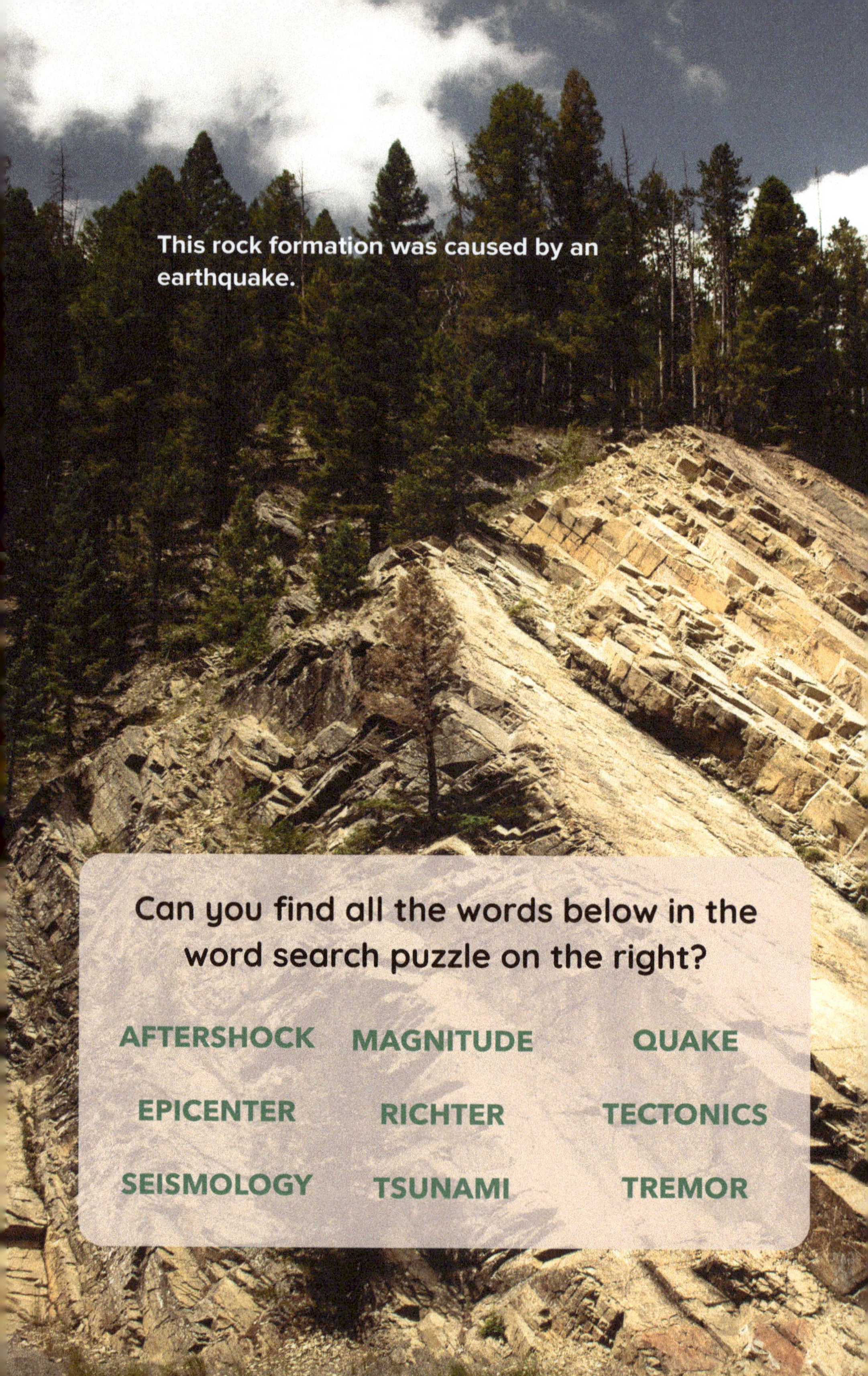

This rock formation was caused by an earthquake.

Can you find all the words below in the word search puzzle on the right?

AFTERSHOCK   MAGNITUDE   QUAKE
EPICENTER   RICHTER   TECTONICS
SEISMOLOGY   TSUNAMI   TREMOR

EARTHQUAKE WORD SEARCH

M A G N I T U D E D S S
B V F U Y E G S C B F E
Z Q S T X T S U N A M I
X G H T E C T O N I C S
C J U T P R C N G D S M
R Q T V I Z S X F P I O
H I W R C G Y H Z X F L
F V C W E Z X J O C S O
D Y I H N M M J G C A G
A Q C X T Z O B S A K Y
Q U A K E E C R C X C X
X N H G R S R A H D S A

SOLUTION

M	A	G	N	I	T	U	D	E			S
		F									E
			T		T	S	U	N	A	M	I
			T	E	C	T	O	N	I	C	S
			P	R							M
R		T		I		S					O
	I		R	C			H				L
		C		E				O			O
			H	N	M				C		G
				T		O				K	Y
Q	U	A	K	E	E		R				
				R		R					

SOURCES

"Tangshan Earthquake Of 1976 | Magnitude, Deaths, Damage, & Facts". 2023. Encyclopedia Britannica. https://www.britannica.com/event/Tangshan-earthquake-of-1976.

"Valdivia Earthquake Strikes Chile". 2023. Education. Nationalgeographic.Org. https://education.nationalgeographic.org/resource/valdivia-earthquake-strikes-chile/.

"Earthquakes". 2023. USGS.gov. https://www.usgs.gov/programs/earthquake-hazards/earthquakes.

"2023 Turkey-Syria Earthquake - Center For Disaster Philanthropy". 2023. Center For Disaster Philanthropy. https://disasterphilanthropy.org/disasters/2023-turkey-syria-earthquake/.

Panchuk, Karla. 2021. "12.3 Earthquakes And Plate Tectonics". Bccampus. https://opentextbc.ca/physicalgeologyh5p/chapter/earthquakes-and-plate-tectonics/.

"Plate Tectonics And The Ring Of Fire". 2023. Education. Nationalgeographic.Org. https://education.nationalgeographic.org/resource/plate-tectonics-ring-fire/.

Fukuji, Tammy. 2023. "How Do Earthquakes Generate Tsunamis? - International Tsunami Information Center". Itic.Ioc-Unesco.Org. http://itic.ioc-unesco. org/index.php?option=com_content&view=article&id=1158&Itemid=2026.

"Japan Earthquake And Tsunami Of 2011 | Facts & Death Toll". 2023. Encyclopedia Britannica. https://www.britannica.com/event/Japan-earthquake-and-tsunami-of-2011.

"Will Future Astronauts Need To Worry About Moonquakes?". 2023. Science Friday. https://www.sciencefriday.com/educational-resources/future-astronauts-moonquakes/.

Sohl, F., and G. Schubert. 2015. "Interior Structure, Composition, And Mineralogy Of The Terrestrial Planets". Treatise On Geophysics, 23-64. doi:10.1016/b978-0-444-53802-4.00166-4.

"Early Warning: GPS Data Could Detect Large Earthquakes Hours Before They Happen". 2023. Scitechdaily. Com. https://scitechdaily.com/early-warning-gps-data-could-detect-large-earthquakes-hours-before-they-happen/.

"Seismometer - Wikipedia". 2014. En.Wikipedia.Org. https://en.wikipedia.org/wiki/Seismometer.

"How Do We Measure Earthquake Magnitude? | Upseis | Michigan Tech". 2023. Michigan Technological University. https://www.mtu.edu/geo/community/seismology/learn/earthquake-measur

GLOSSARY

AFTERSHOCK: Smaller earthquakes that follow the main earthquake.

ASTHENOSPHERE: The semi-fluid layer beneath the lithosphere on which tectonic plates float.

CONVERGENT BOUNDARY: The area where two tectonic plates come together, often resulting in one plate being forced under the other in a process called subduction.

CRUST: The outermost layer of the Earth, composed of a variety of rocks. It's where we live and where all earthquakes occur.

DIVERGENT BOUNDARY: The place where two tectonic plates move away from each other, allowing magma to rise and form new crust.

EPICENTER: The point on the Earth's surface directly above where an earthquake starts.

FAULTLINE: A fracture or zone of fractures between two blocks of rock.

HYPOCENTER: Also known as the focus. It's the exact point inside the Earth where an earthquake begins.

LIQUEFACTION: When saturated soil substantially loses strength and stiffness due to applied stress, such as during an earthquake, causing it to behave like a liquid.

LITHOSPHERE: The rigid outer layer of the Earth, consisting of the crust and upper mantle.

MAGNITUDE: A measure of the size or energy released during an earthquake.

P-WAVE: Primary wave, or compression wave, is the fastest type of seismic wave. It causes particles in the ground to move in a push-pull motion parallel to the direction the wave is moving.

PLATEAU: An area of relatively high ground. In the context of earthquakes, they can be uplifted due to tectonic activity.

RICHTER SCALE: A logarithmic scale used to measure the strength or magnitude of an earthquake.

SEISMIC: Relating to earthquakes or other vibrations of the Earth and its crust.

SEISMOGRAPH: An instrument that measures and records details of earthquakes, such as force and duration.

S-WAVE: Secondary wave, or shear wave, is the second-fastest seismic wave. It causes particles in the ground to move perpendicular to the direction the wave is moving.

SUBDUCTION: The process by which one tectonic plate moves under another and sinks into the mantle as the plates converge.

TECTONIC PLATES: Large pieces of the Earth's crust that fit together like a puzzle to make up the Earth's surface.

TRANSFORM BOUNDARY: The place where two tectonic plates slide past each other.

TREMOR: A non-rhythmic, low-force shaking movement. Tremors are often associated with earthquakes.

TSUNAMI: A series of ocean waves with very long wavelengths typically caused by large-scale disturbances of the ocean, such as earthquakes occurring beneath the sea floor.

Thanks for joining us on this exciting journey through the world of earthquakes! If you enjoyed this book, please consider leaving a review—they always make us smile, and help other readers find great books to read!

You might also like:

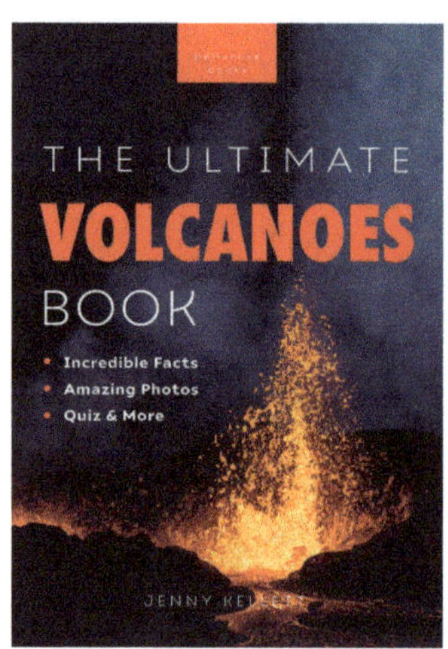

For more great books, just scan the QR code below, or visit us at:

www.bellanovabooks.com